✦Jane Goodall's✦
ANIMAL WORLD

LIONS

by Leslie MacGuire

Scientific Consultants: Roger Caras and Craig Packer
Photographs by Leonard Lee Rue III and Len Rue, Jr.

Collins

◇ Introduction: The Lion by Jane Goodall

When you watch a huge black-maned lion standing on the African plains, outlined in gold by the setting sun, and hear his great roar filling the air, you know exactly why the lion has always been known as the King of Beasts. And when you lie in bed in a small tent out in the winds of Africa and hear lions calling back and forth to each other, the sound is truly awe-inspiring. I shall never forget the night a lion roared about five feet from the thin canvas wall of my tent. The ground seemed to shake with the sound – I certainly shook!

The first lion I saw in the wild was way back in 1957 when I was working for Dr Louis Leakey at Olduvai Gorge in Tanzania. One evening, after digging for fossils all day, I was taking an evening walk with the other assistant when we heard a low growl. I looked around – and there was a lion standing about thirty feet away and staring at us. I decided that we should move very slowly across the gorge and climb out onto the open plains. It was obviously the right thing to do. The lion followed us for about fifty yards and then seemed to lose interest.

I shall always remember the first time I was really close to a hunting lioness. I watched as she crept towards the grazing Thompson's gazelle she had singled out. She made use of every tiny piece of vegetation and froze, motionless, whenever he raised his head. When she finally reckoned she was close enough for a kill, she charged straight towards it. I was filled with awe at her power, speed and ferocity, her great size, and her rippling muscles. On that occasion the prey got away and I was pleased. But like other meat-eaters, lions have to hunt and kill in order to survive. And when once, I saw some little cubs who were starving to death during a scorching dry summer, I longed for their mother to be successful in the hunt.

Only the human animal kills just for "fun". Hunters sometimes shoot lions just so that they can stuff those majestic heads and hang them on their walls. Fortunately, today there are many parks and reserves where lions can live out their lives without any interference from humans. In this book you will learn more about this magnificent animal. The more we know about lions, the better we can respect and understand them.

◇ Contents

Where Do Lions Live?	4
The Family Tree of the Lion	6
The Lion Community	7
Sizing Up the Lion	9
How Lions Move	11
The Senses of the Lion	13
How Lions Communicate	15
Being Born	16
Growing Up	18
Living Day to Day	22
Lions in Captivity	30
Protecting the Lions	31

◇ Where Do Lions Live?

Lions today live on the plains and in the woodlands of Africa. About two thousand years ago they were found wild in southern Europe, and until the 1930s in the Middle East and India as well. But they were gradually hunted to extinction in these places, except for a very small number in India, all in a preserve called the Gir Forest. Now most lions live in game preserves, where they are protected from hunters. The biggest of these preserves is the Serengeti National Park in Tanzania, which covers 14,763 square kilometres.

Lions survive by hunting grass-eating animals or *herbivores* like the wildebeest, gazelle, zebra, and buffalo. They compete with meat-eaters like the hyena and wild dog for the herbivores. Meat-eating birds such as vultures pick the bones of the prey clean after the predators have finished with them. Only some grass-eaters, like the adult elephant and rhinoceros, are so big and powerful that they are nearly always safe from lions.

There are two seasons in Africa, the dry season and the rainy

EUROPE

MIDDLE EAST

AFRICA
Distribution of lion
(shaded area)

River Nile

River Niger

Lake Victoria

River Congo

Serengeti National Park

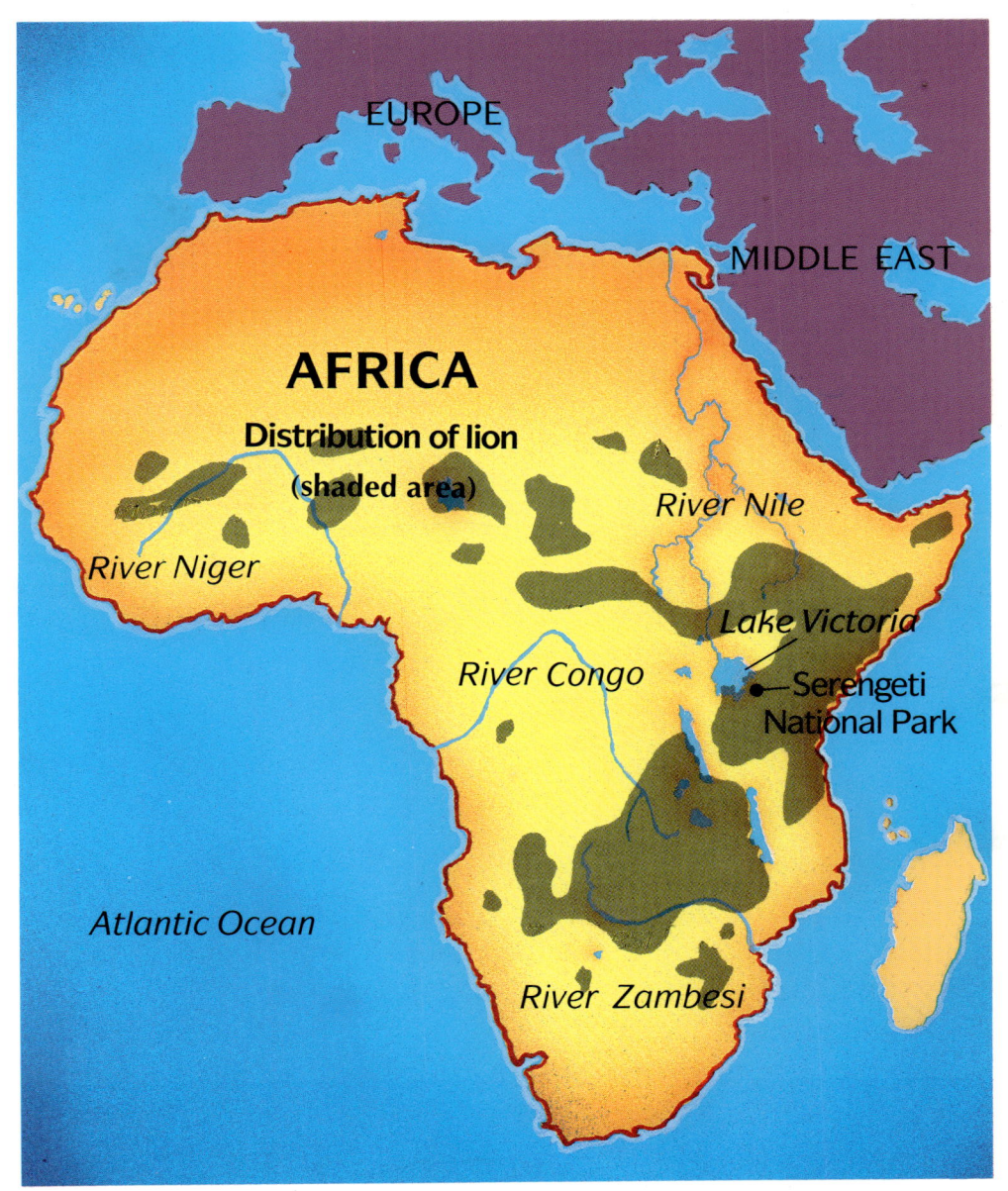

Atlantic Ocean

River Zambesi

season. During the rainy season, many of the grass-eaters, like the wildebeest and zebra, migrate to the plains. During the dry season, they move back to the woodlands. Groups of lions, who live in one place throughout the year, must find other kinds of animals to hunt when the migrating animals move away. Lions who don't live in groups often follow the herds.

◇ The Family Tree of the Lion

This is the evolutionary family tree of the lion. Today's animals are depicted on the top branches of the tree.

Lions have the scientific name *Panthera leo* (pan-*ther*-ra *lee*-o). They are members of the cat family, which can be divided into two main groups. There are big cats that roar: the lion, tiger, jaguar, and leopard. There are the medium-sized and small cats that don't roar, including the ocelot, lynx, puma, small wild cats, and, of course, the house cat. The cheetah occupies its own special branch of the cat family tree.

Cats are descended from small, insect-eating mammals called Miacidae (my-*ee*-ci-dee) that roamed the earth 190 million years ago. Starting about forty million years ago, one branch of the insect-eaters gradually evolved into cats. One type of cat, the sabre-toothed cat or *Smilodon*, became extinct about ten thousand years ago.

◇ The Lion Community

Lions live in groups, called *prides*. There may be one to eighteen adult females in a pride, with their cubs, and one to nine adult males. The females are generally all related, and have been born and reared in the same pride. But the males are transient, and may live with one pride for only a short time.

Lions usually hunt in groups, but sometimes only one lioness in the pride will go hunting. Generally, it is the lionesses who hunt. After a successful kill the males join the females and typically claim the "lion's share" of the meat. In fact, a hunting male can be spotted more easily by the prey because of his mane – the lionesses have an easier time without him.

There is no definite leader in a pride. When they are on the move, one or more females will usually lead the group. A male may follow behind the cubs. Except for small fights now and then, lions in a pride get along very well. They are quite affectionate, and lick or rub up against each other whenever they meet. Often they rest in contact with each other.

Lion prides have special ranges or territories, which males and females both defend against strange lions. Lions mark their territory with the smell of their urine or dung.

The lions know their territory well. They know the best hunting and drinking areas. Lions move to different parts of their territory during the year, depending on where the most prey can be found. Female lions also know the safest places in their territory to hide their cubs and protect them from harm.

A pride's territory can be anywhere from 20 square kilometres to 389 square kilometres in size. The less food, the bigger the territory must be. Sometimes these territories overlap.

Not all lions belong to a pride. All young males are forced out of their prides by the adult males. Often they travel with their brothers or with other solitary males. The strongest will drive older males from neighbouring prides and take over their females. Eventually they in turn will be driven from the pride by younger males, and forced to roam on their own. Some young lionesses are also forced out and form new prides with their sisters.

Lions have a much better chance of surviving if they belong to a pride. Without companions, they might be killed by larger groups of neighbouring lions.

◇ Sizing Up the Lion

A fully grown African lion is about three metres long and weighs about 227 kilograms. The only cat alive today that is bigger than the lion is the tiger. Siberian tigers are 3.7 metres long, and can weigh as much as 318 kilograms. The female lion, or lioness, is much smaller, weighing only about 136 kilograms. For comparison, the average house cat weighs about 4.5 kilograms and is about 0.4 metres long.

One thing that sets most male lions apart from all other cats is the ruff of hair, or mane that grows thickly on their heads and necks. This mane gives the lion an impressive, even regal, appearance. It makes the male look even bigger than he is, and protects his neck during fights with other males. The mane has helped earn him the nickname "King of the Beasts". However, he does not really rule supreme. He will run from both elephant and rhinoceros.

Cheetah
2.1 metres
(7 feet)

Sabre-toothed Cat
2.4 metres
(8 feet)

Siberian Tiger
3.7 metres
(12 feet)

Lynx
0.9 metres
(3 feet)

Lion
2.7 metres
(9 feet)

Domestic Cat
0.4 metres
(15 inches)

Measurement:
head-plus-body length

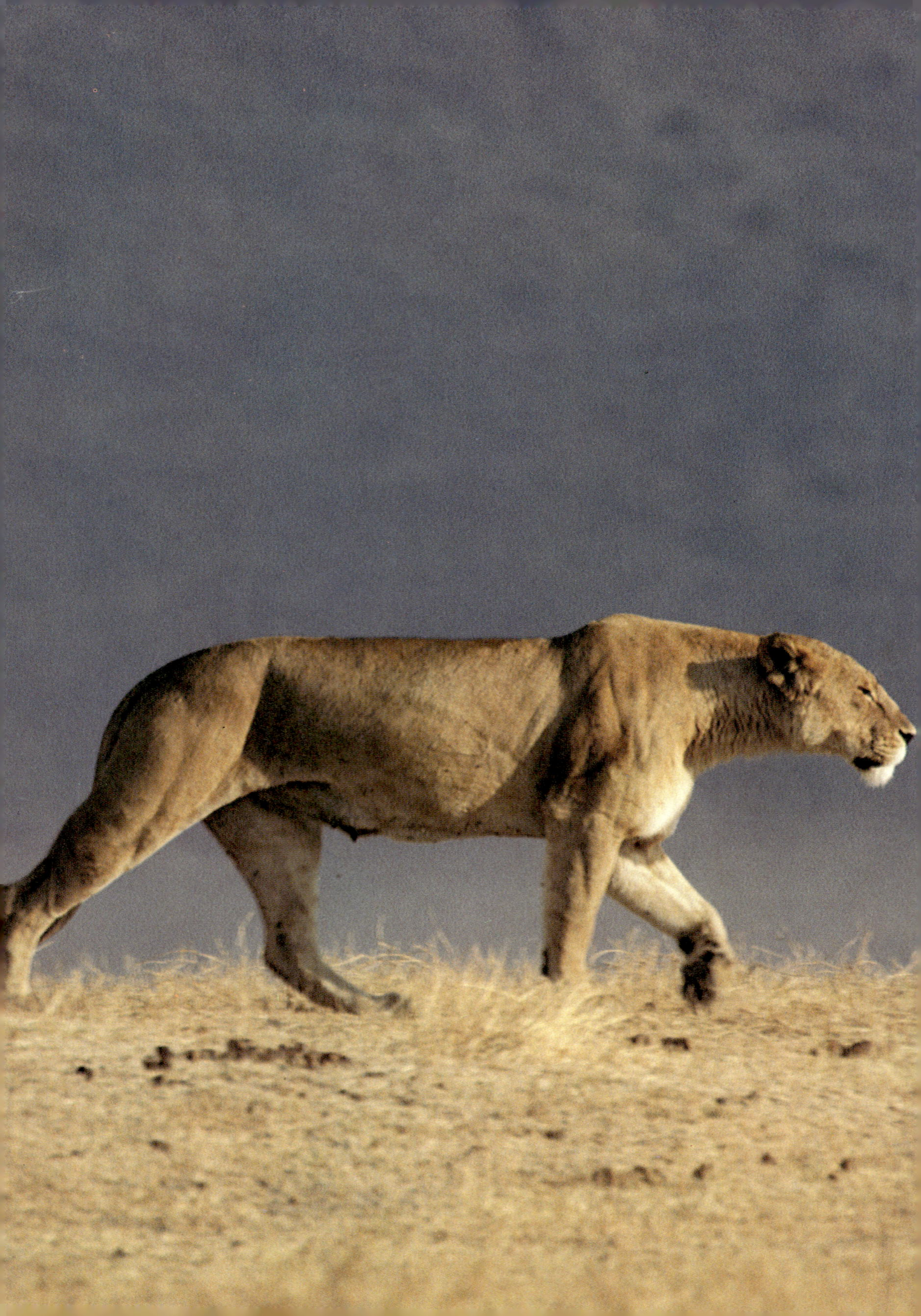

◇ How Lions Move

Lion's bodies are long and slender. Their bones aren't very big but they are very heavy. Powerful muscles hold these bones loosely together. It is this loose structure that makes the movement of the lion appear so fluid.

In order to survive, lions must be able to stalk and kill their prey. A lioness who is hunting moves slowly. When she spots suitable prey, she crouches low, then uses every bit of cover – grass, bushes, and so on – as she creeps closer and closer to the unsuspecting animal. Once she is close, she bounds forward, very fast. If she catches her prey she leaps up, digs into the animal's shoulder or rump with her powerful claws, then uses her weight to drag the animal down. Then she hangs onto the throat and strangles it.

Ordinarily, a lion walks in a relaxed manner. But when it is hunting, it holds its body rigid and stares right at possible prey. When it starts to stalk, it crouches low to the ground and strains its head forward. When it is angry, it lashes its tail back and forth. A mother lioness raises her tail and flicks it in the air so her cubs can follow her through high grass.

◇ The Senses of the Lion

Lions use their senses for receiving messages from prey as well as from other lions.

Their eyes are at the front of their faces, just like those of humans. This makes lions good at judging distances. Lions can see small objects easily. A vulture circling far in the distance may look like a tiny black speck in the sky to us. To a lion, that speck may mean an easy meal. If the vulture spirals rapidly downwards, the lion knows it is waiting for a sick animal to die, or has spotted one already dead. Lions, like hyenas, are willing to scavenge as well as hunt.

A lion's sense of smell is better than that of humans. Lions get a lot of information from what they smell. They can tell if a strange lion is in the area. They can track one of their own pride. They can tell if prey is nearby and approximately how long ago the animal has passed.

Lions also have very good hearing. They can hear the sounds made by other animals from very far away. Their ears move, so that they can focus easily on sounds coming from any direction.

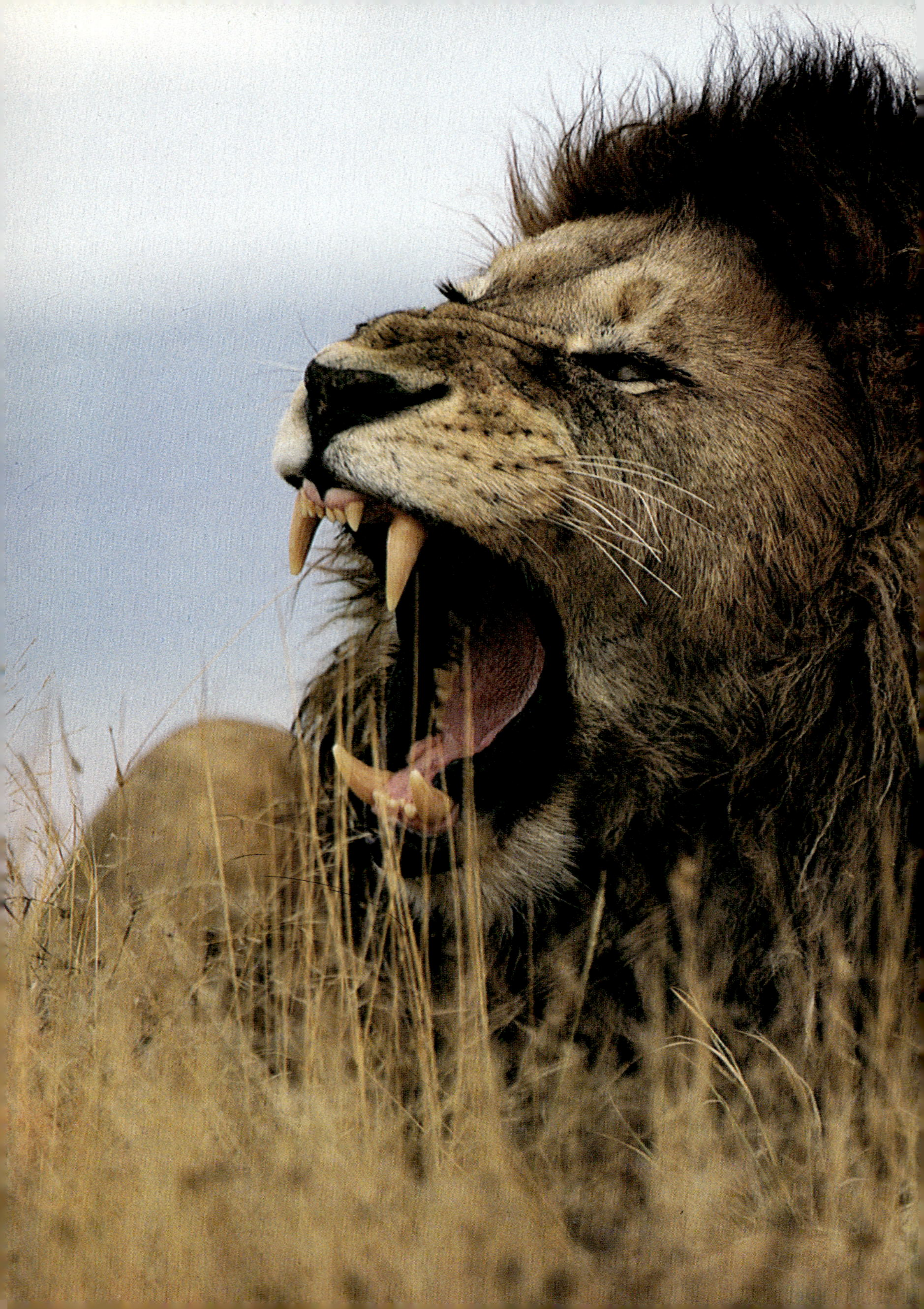

◇ How Lions Communicate

Lions communicate with their whole bodies, but especially with their faces. Their facial expressions change when they are angry, startled, frightened or content.

Lions also make different noises that mean different things. They snarl when they're attacking another animal and when they're on the defensive. Cubs will meow when they are lost. But the roar is the lion's most characteristic sound. Lionesses looking for their cubs will give a soft roar. A full roar means that lions are trying to communicate over longer distances. The roar can help them find each other. It can help mark territory. Or, when members of a pride roar at the same time, it can help bring them together as a group.

◇ Being Born

Lions start mating between the ages of three and four. When they are mating, a male and female will stay together for three or four days. They rarely hunt during this time.

If a female gets pregnant, the cubs are born three and a half months later. When the mother lioness is ready to give birth, she leaves the pride and finds a hidden place where she has her cubs. Usually there are two to four cubs in a litter. At first the cubs weigh only between one and two kilograms, and, like domestic kittens, are so weak and uncoordinated they can barely crawl. Their eyes are still shut tight. After ten days to two weeks, they open them for the first time.

From the moment they are born, lion cubs are in danger. Their mothers must leave them to go hunting – sometimes for a day or more. Other meat-eaters (even male lions) may find, kill and eat them. Only about half the cubs born live to grow up.

By the time the cubs are about six weeks old, their mothers bring them back to live with the pride. They are no longer so helpless, and there is less chance the other lions in the pride will hurt them. If more than one lioness in the pride has cubs, the mothers help each other feed and take care of them.

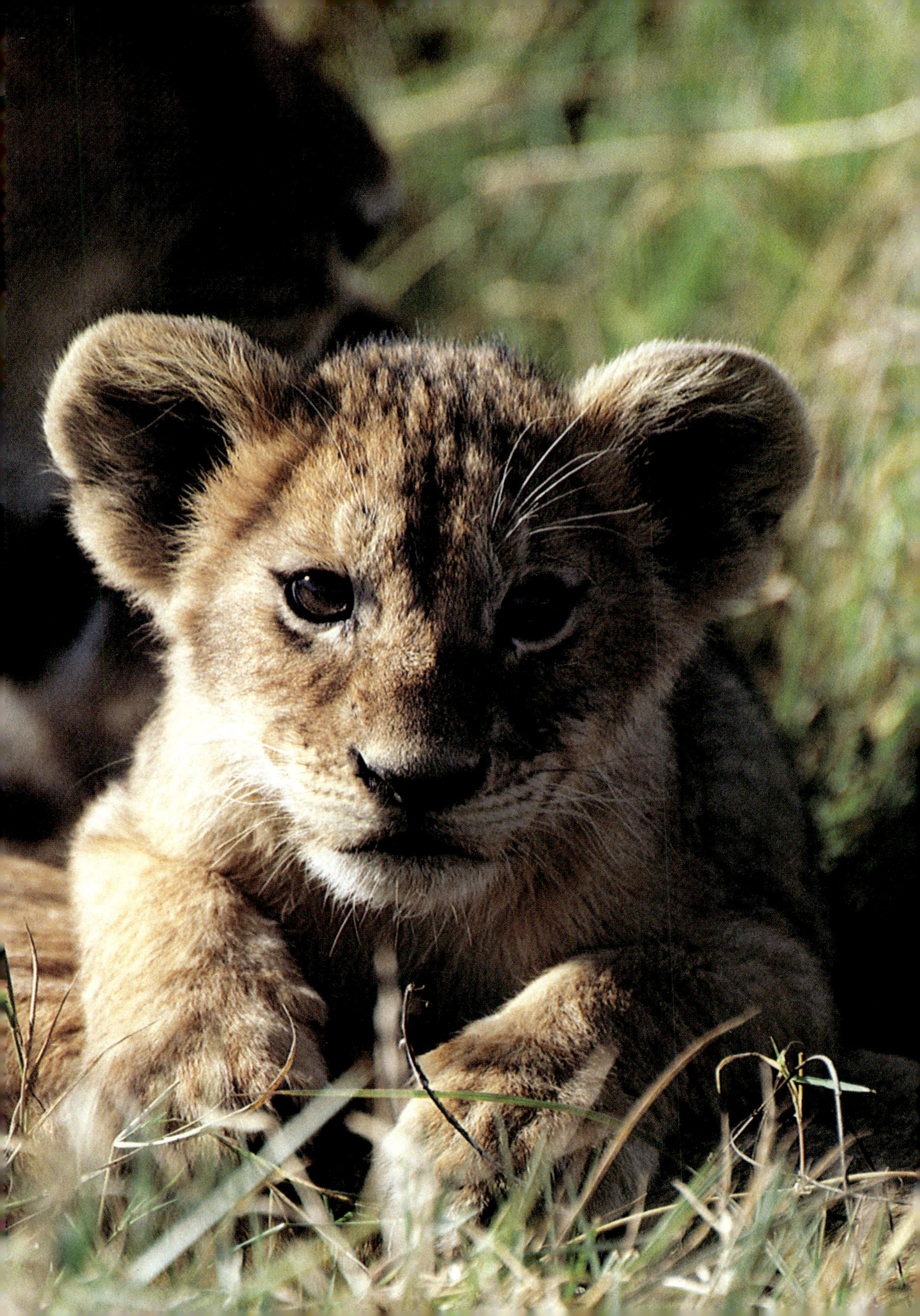

◇ Growing Up

A lioness moves her newborn cubs by picking them up gently in her mouth and carrying them. At about three weeks, the cubs are able to walk, and at about six weeks, they start to follow their mothers to the hunt. They then taste meat for the first time. During this weaning period, they continue to drink their mothers' milk as well. Males, being the biggest and strongest lions, usually get most of the meat at a kill, but lions do not actually eat in a set order. There is often a struggle over the body of the prey. Cubs sometimes end up eating last – or not at all.

As they get older, the lion cubs also start playing. During play the cubs learn much about adult behaviour. They pounce, and

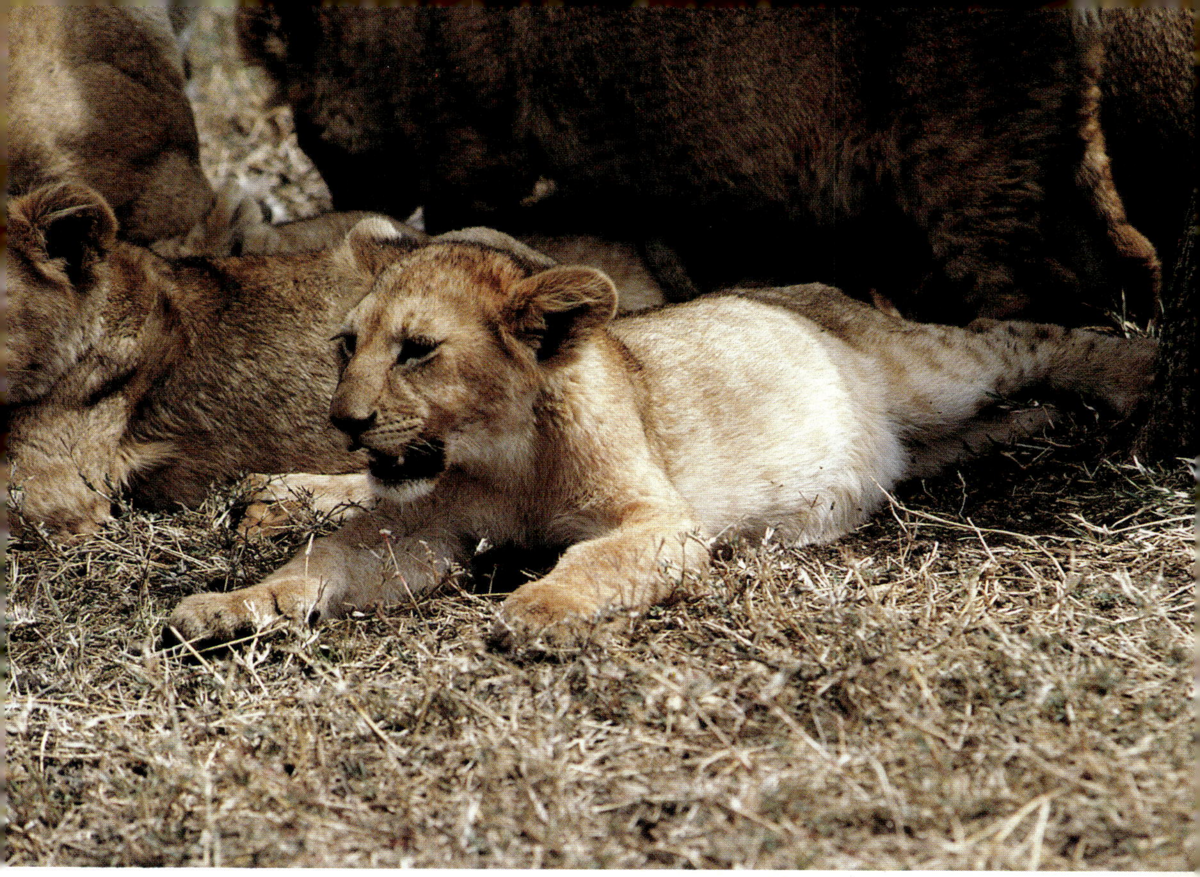
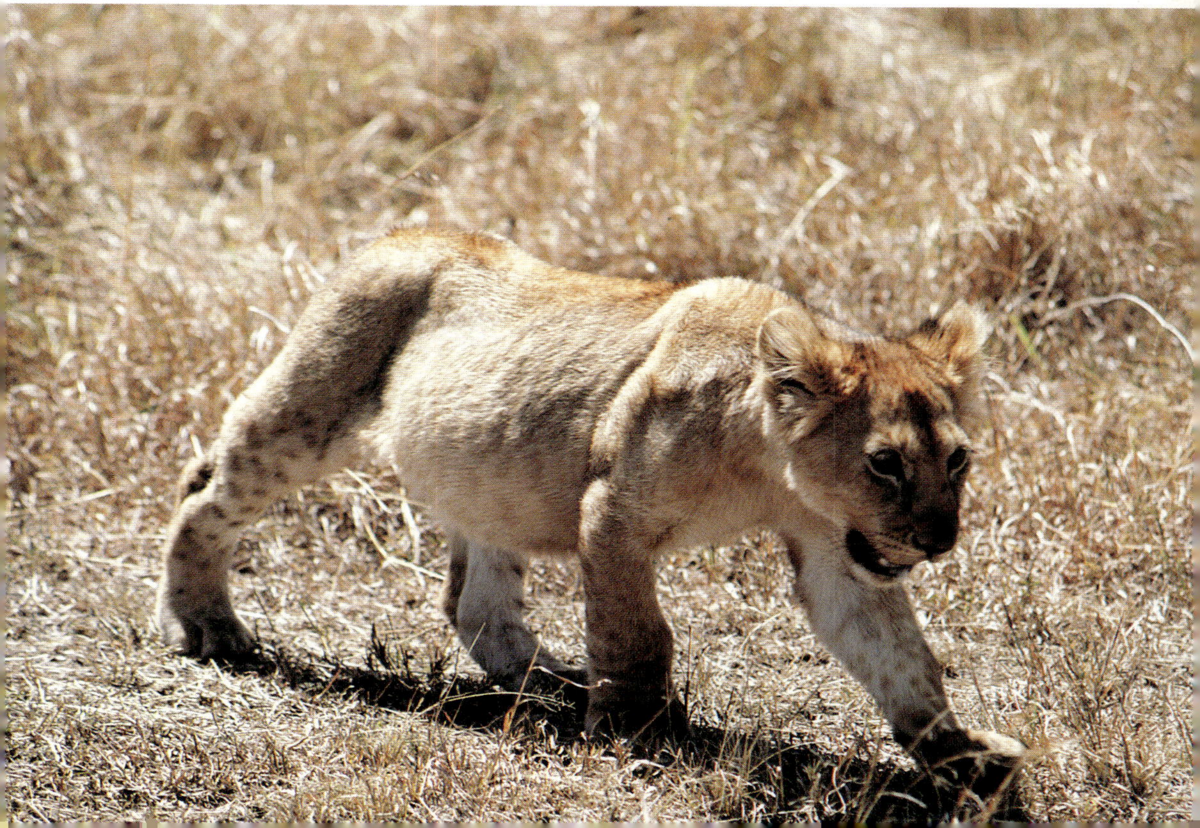

leap, and chase each other all around. They attack the tufts of hair at the end of their mothers' tails. They drag sticks back and forth along the ground, just the way the adults drag the animals they have killed. And they start to make all the different movements and calls that are typical of adult lions.

At fifteen months cubs lose their baby teeth and grow their adult teeth, including their big canines. These will enable them to catch and kill prey. Often by the time males are about eighteen months old, their fathers are driven out by a new set of males and the sub-adults are driven out too. Females will probably remain and help the other adults to hunt.

Lions can live to be fifteen to eighteen years old in the wild.

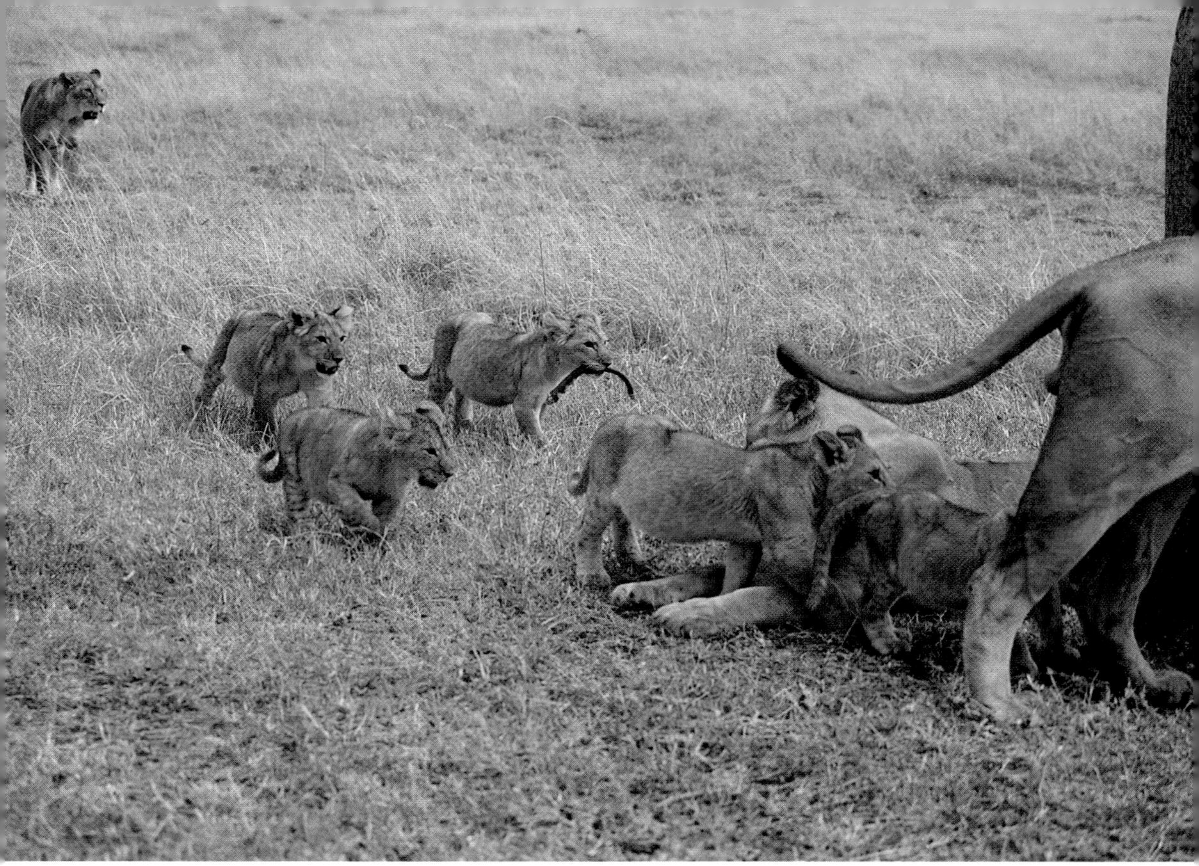

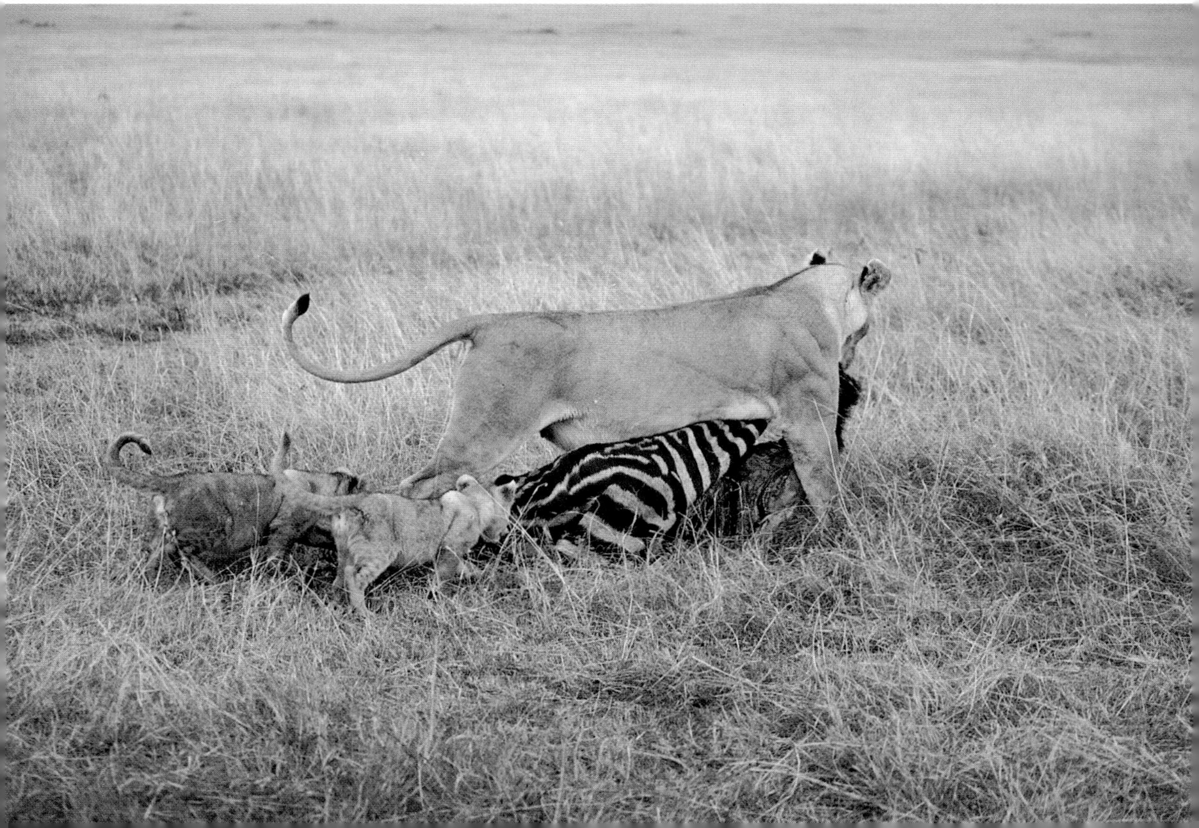

◇ Living Day to Day

It is late afternoon in the Serengeti, and the lion pride has been resting in the shade of an acacia tree all day. The male is lashing his tail, trying to find some relief from the biting flies. Two lionesses sleep together, some cubs curled up beside them.

Soon the mother lioness wakes up. Leaving her cubs behind, she wanders off looking for prey. She sees some Thomsons gazelle grazing nearby. But when her two cubs come bounding up, the gazelle are startled and take off through the tall, waving grass.

A bit further along, a warthog snorts and paws at the ground. The lioness rushes at it from behind, but the warthog dives into its underground burrow and disappears completely.

The lioness returns to the pride and nurses the cubs for a while. When they start to play with her ears, she nuzzles them back.

About an hour later, the lions hear howling in the distance. A pack of hyenas has just made a kill. The two females take off in the direction of the sound. Sometimes it is easier for lions to chase hyenas away and steal their kill than to hunt for themselves.

But when the lionesses approach the fallen wildebeest, the hyenas band together to defend their meal. The lionesses finally give up and head back to their resting place.

After another nap, the lionesses decide to go hunting again. First they stop at a waterhole to drink and watch for prey. It has been two days since they last had any water, but sometimes they go for nine days without drinking. Tonight they have the waterhole to themselves.

About a quarter of a mile away, the two lionesses find a herd of zebra. One lioness circles slowly around the herd and finally hides herself in some tall grasses just to the east. Meanwhile, the other lioness lowers herself into a crouch. She singles out a young animal that seems to be straggling behind the rest and begins to stalk. When she is close enough, she breaks into a run. The startled zebra sprints off – straight towards the mother lioness. Suddenly bursting out of her hiding place in the grass, the mother lioness pounces at the zebra and brings it down.

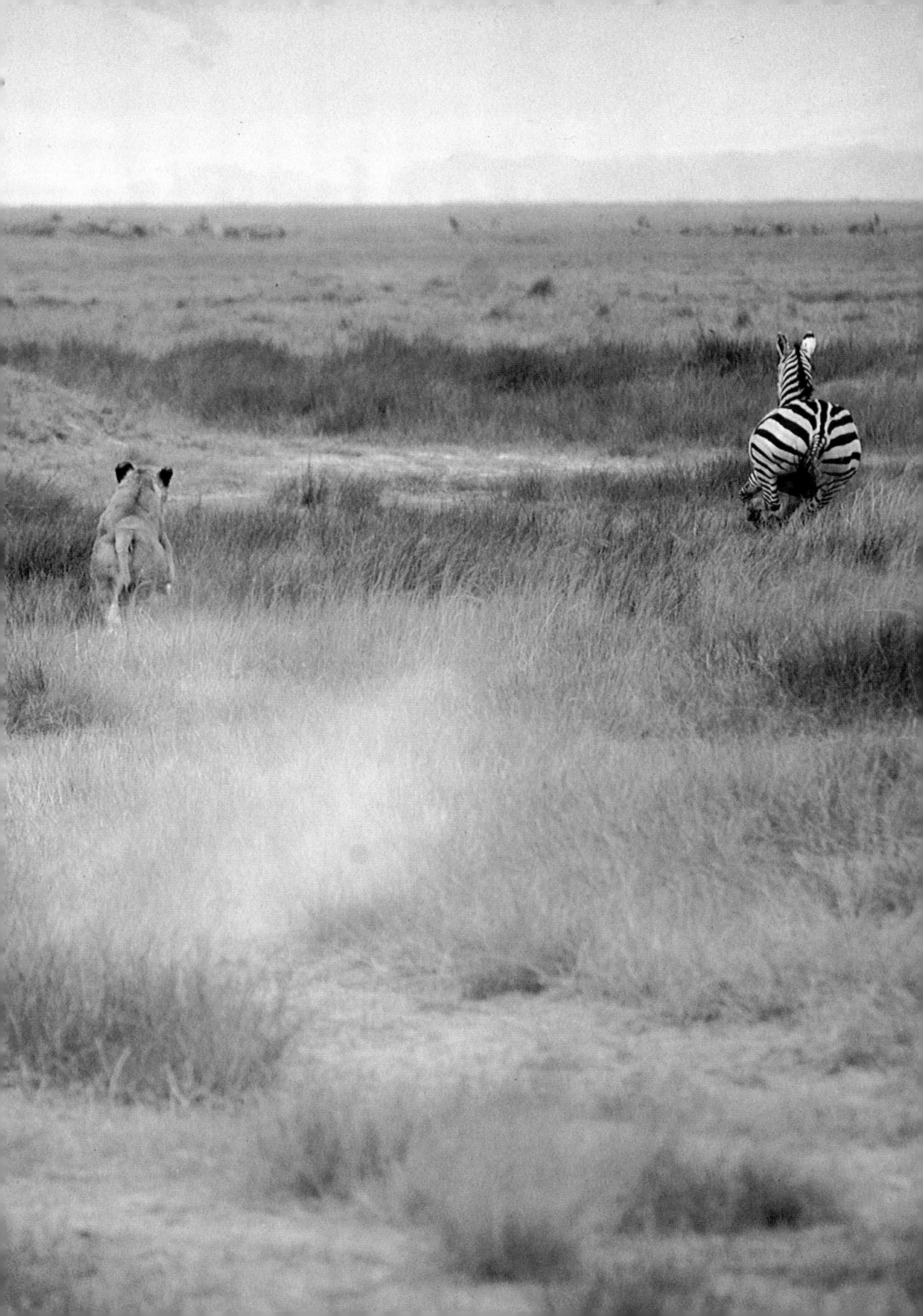

For a while now, the male and the cubs have been walking slowly behind the lionesses. When they hear the sounds of the kill, they run up to eat. It takes more than four hours to finish the meal. There is plenty to eat. Everyone has his fill.

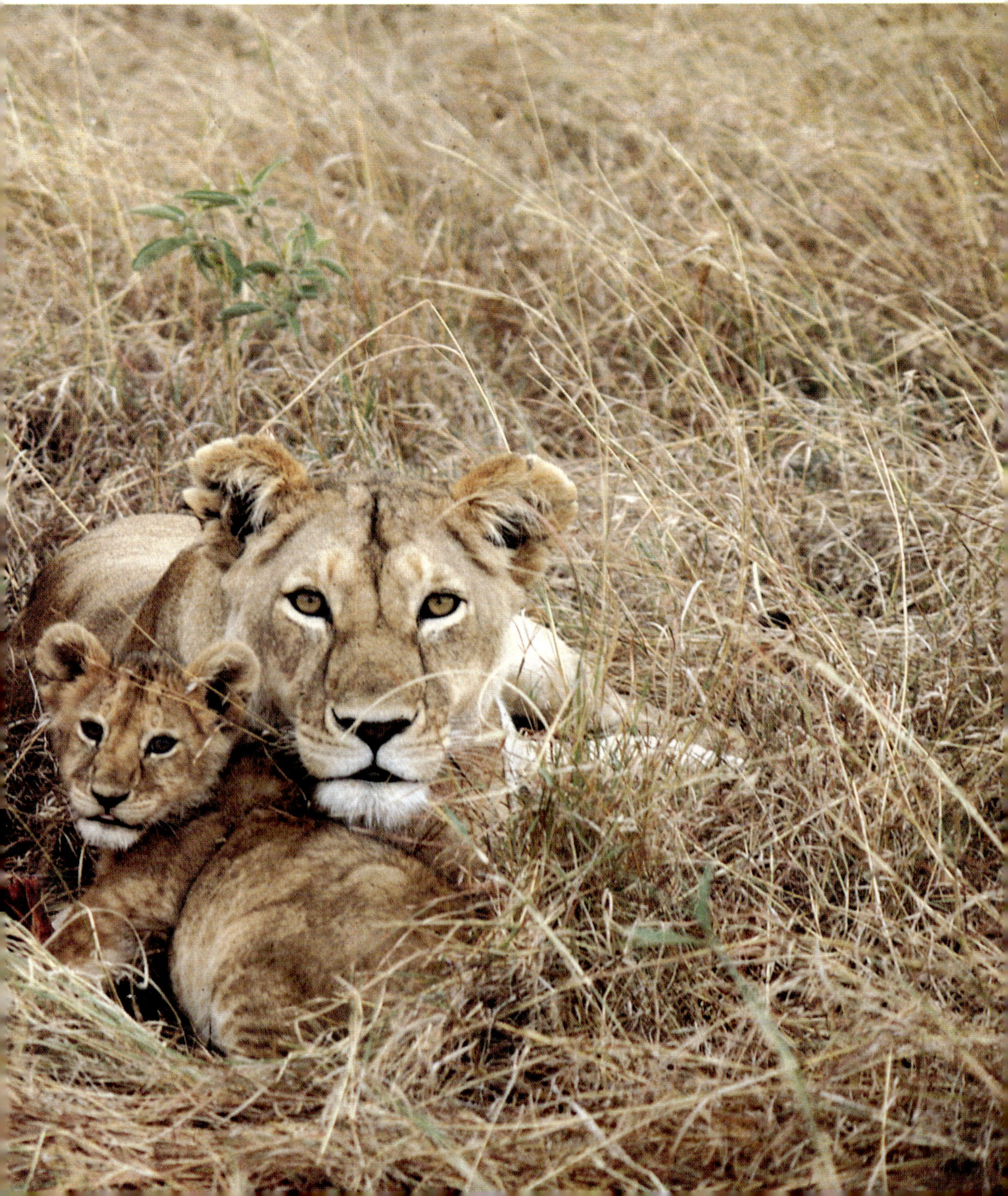

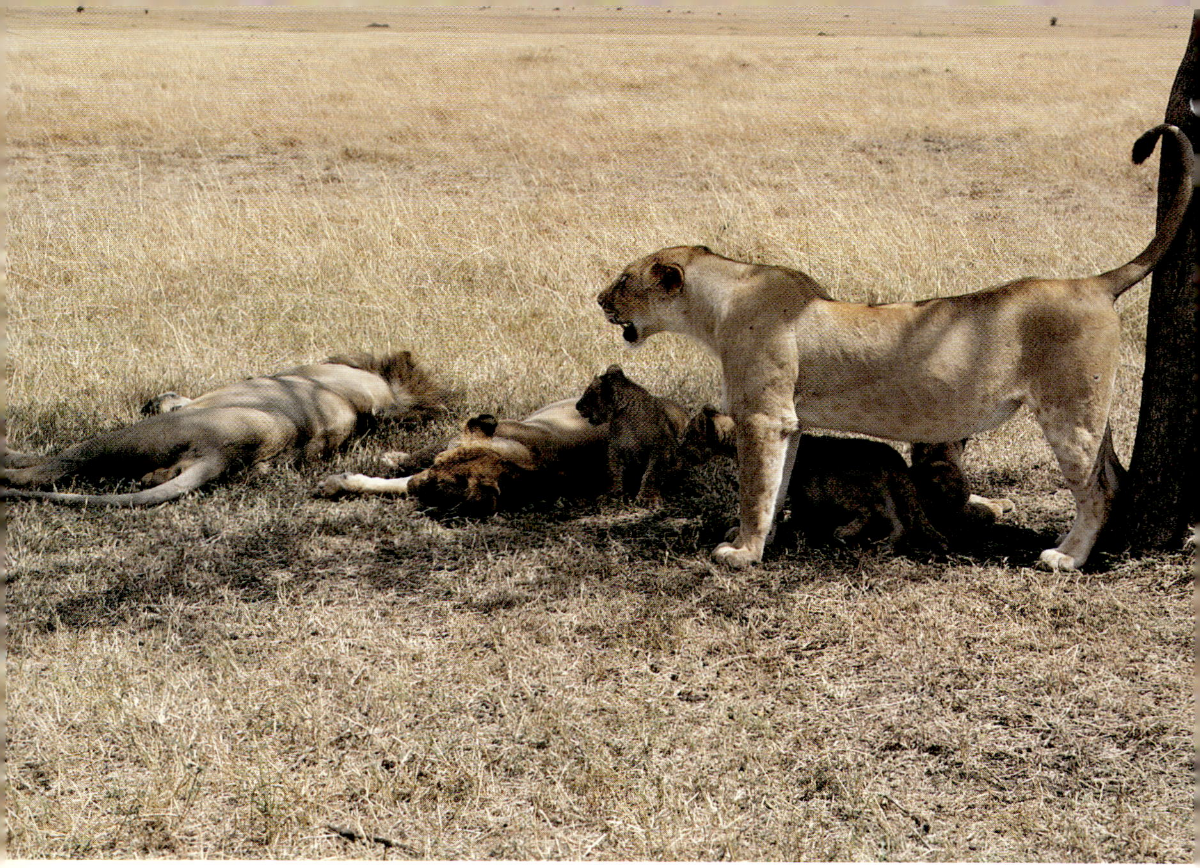

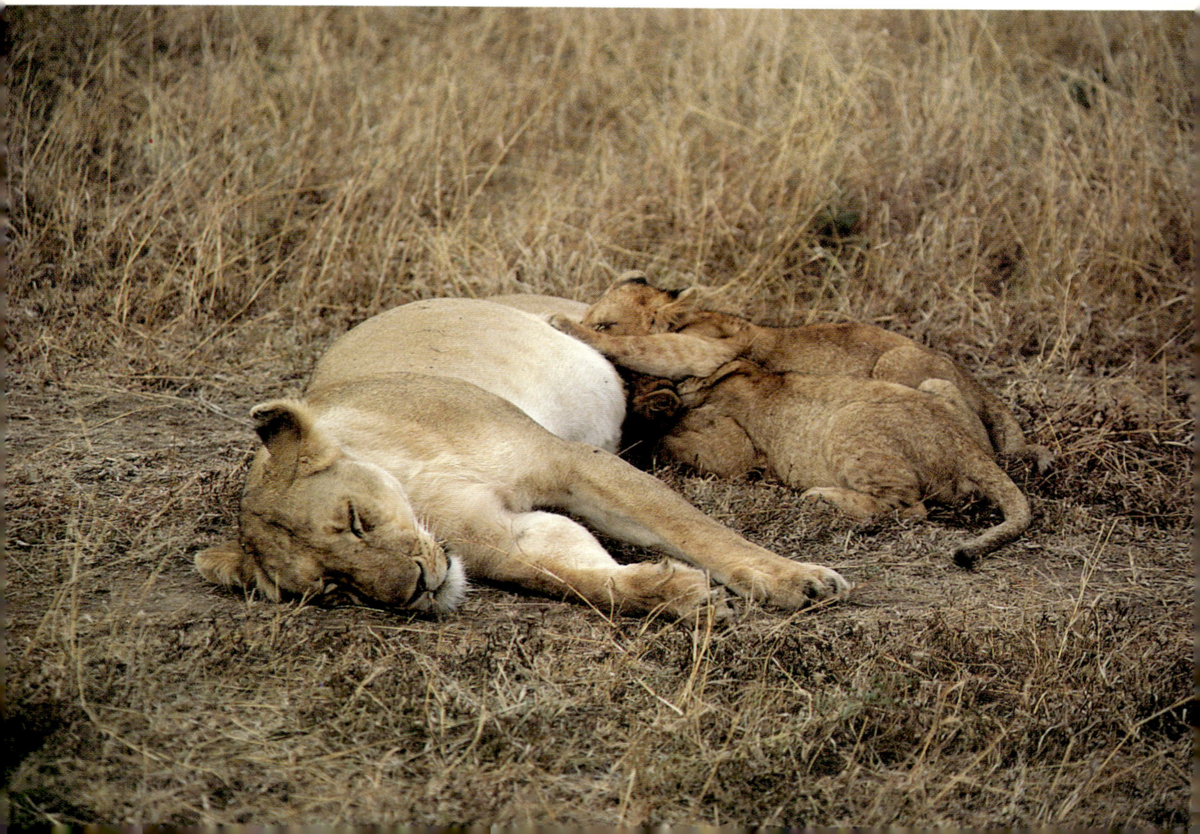

By now, it's starting to get warm. The lions are full and drowsy. The cubs follow behind the adults until they find a good shade tree to rest under. Then they all settle down. The cubs nurse for a while, then the lions fall asleep.

In one full day, the pride has spent about nineteen hours resting and five hours fully awake and active. The lionesses have walked about four kilometres. Although he usually averages about six-and-a-half kilometres a day, today the male has walked only about one. This was a particularly quiet day for him, and a good day for the pride.

◇ Lions in Captivity

Although lions have been very popular members of zoos for many years, they have not always been well treated. Great advances have recently been made in keeping zoo lions healthy and content. In fact, African lions have been doing so well in captivity that zoos have been limiting the number of babies they have.

Cement cages may be easy to clean, but they are too small and cramped for the lion. Many zoos are now building much more natural enclosures, even setting aside large outdoor areas for lions to roam in. Zoos also used to make the mistake of feeding their lions a soft meat diet. But the animals weren't getting enough of the vitamins, minerals, and calcium they would get in their normal diet. That's because big cats eat the entire animal, including the bones and contents of the stomach.

Now, more zoos make sure that lions live healthy lives even when in captivity.

◇ Protecting the Lions

One member of the lion family, the Asian lion, is endangered in the wild. Only about 200 of them survive in a reserve in the Gir Forest in India. As a result, there is now a special Asian lion breeding programme at the San Diego Zoo. Two prides have been created, with almost twenty lions obtained from other zoos.

It is extremely difficult to get an accurate count of lions. They move about during the night, they shift from pride to pride, and they live across very large areas. There are currently about 2,500 lions living in the Serengeti National Park.

Even on the game preserves, lions can be endangered. Lions have few natural enemies in the wild. But they are often caught in poachers' snares, and sometimes still killed by hunters, although hunting lions has been banned in most of Africa. When they leave the bounds of the preserve and roam into farming areas, lions risk being killed because they are a threat to cattle.

Because lions are able to live on the preserves and in zoos, they are not now in danger of extinction. But they need continued protection if their survival is to be ensured.

About the Contributors

JANE GOODALL was born in London on April 3, 1934, and grew up in Bournemouth, on the south coast of England. In 1960, she began studying chimpanzees in the wild in Gombe, Tanzania. After receiving her doctorate in ethology at Cambridge University, Dr Goodall founded the Gombe Stream Research Centre for the study of chimpanzees and baboons. In 1977, she established the Jane Goodall Institute for Wildlife Research, Education and Conservation to promote animal research throughout the world. She has written three books for adults, including the bestseller *In the Shadow of Man*, and three books for children, including the recent *My Life With the Chimpanzees* and *The Chimpanzee Family Book*.

LESLIE MACGUIRE is a former children's book editor and the author of over a hundred books for children, including *Growing Up in Nature* and *Animal Helpers*. She lives in southern California, where she is a full-time writer.

Jane Goodall's commitment to the animal world is expressed in her words, "Only when we understand can we care. Only when we care can we help. Only when we help shall they be saved." You can learn more about joining in her efforts to protect endangered wildlife by contacting The Jane Goodall Institute for Wildlife Research, Education, and Conservation, 1601 W. Anklam Road, Tucson, Arizona 85745.

First published in Great Britain 1990 by William Collins, Sons Co. Ltd, 8 Grafton Street, London W1X 3LA.

First published in the United States 1990 by Atheneum.

Copyright © 1990 Byron Preiss Visual Publications Inc.

Introduction © 1990 Jane Goodall.

All rights reserved. No part of this book may be reproduced transmitted in any form or by any means, electronic or mechanic including photocopying, recording, or by any information stora system without permission of the Publisher.

A CIP record for this book is available from the British Library.

ISBN 0 00 184589 6 (hardback)
      0 00 184721 X (paperback)

Printed and bound in Hong Kong by
C&C Offset Printing Co. Ltd.

Cover photo copyright © by Leonard Lee Rue, III.
Back cover photo copyright © by Len Rue, III.
Front cover photo insert of Jane Goodall by Hugo Van Lawic copyright © National Geographic Society
Introduction photo of Jane Goodall copyright © Ben Asen
Interior illustrations copyright © 1989 by Byron Preiss Visu Publications, Inc.

Interior photos copyright © Leonard Lee Rue III and Len Rue, J except for the following: page 30: copyright © New York Zoologic Society.

Interior illustrations by Ralph Reese
Map by Rurick Tyler

Special thanks to Judy Wilson, Jonathan Lanman, Judy Johnso Roger Caras, Bonnie Dalzell, and Dr Craig Packer.

Editor: Ruth Ashby
Associate Editor: Gwendolyn Smith
Cover design: Ted Mader & Associates
Interior design: Alex Jay/Studio J.